Watch Bands!

Turn an ordinary watch into an extraordinary time-piece by making a beaded band! Use our colors or pick beads that match a favorite outfit.

Amethyst Watch - MATERIALS: Amethyst Assortment glass beads • Amethyst mini pony beads • 8 Silver metal drum beads • 6 Silver metal 2.5mm x 6mm spacer beads • Silver watch • Silver toggle clasp • 2 Silver crimp beads • 2 Silver coil crimps • 4 Silver spacer bars • 20 gauge Silver wire • Tiger tail • Wire cutters • Crimp pliers

TIPS: Remove watchband. Place coil crimps over watch spring pins. Replace pins in watch. On both sides of watch, thread and center 12" of tiger tail through coil crimps. Loop 12" of tiger tail over center of coil crimps, center tiger tail and pull down into coils. Treat the 2 center pieces of tiger tail as one strand. Thread beads in a random pattern placing 2 spacer bars on each side of watch. Complete each strand with a mini pony bead. To finish each side of watch, bring the 3 strands of tiger tail together and thread through a metal drum bead. Attach tiger tail to clasp with a crimp bead.

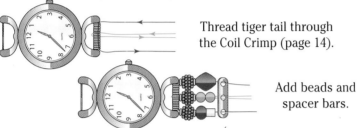

Thread tiger tail through the Coil Crimp (page 14).

Add beads and spacer bars.

Thread tiger tail through clasp then back through crimp bead. Secure crimp bead. Hide tail in beads.

Blue & Green Watch - MATERIALS: 8 Dark Blue and Green striped square glass beads • Blue Assortment glass beads (10 Dark Blue, ¼" square) • 8 Silver metal 7mm round spacer beads • 2 Silver crimp breads • 12mm Silver lobster claw clasp • 6mm Silver split ring • 2 Silver coil crimps • 20 gauge Silver wire • Tiger tail • Wire cutters • Crimp pliers

TIPS: Remove watchband. Place coil crimps over watch spring pins. Replace pins in watch. Loop 12" of tiger tail over coil crimps, center and pull down into coils. Treat the 2 pieces of tiger tail as one strand. Thread beads on tiger tail. Attach tiger tail to clasp and split ring with crimp beads.

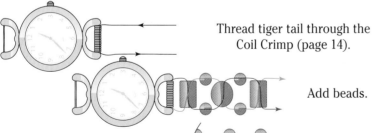

Thread tiger tail through the Coil Crimp (page 14).

Add beads.

Thread tiger tail through clasp then back through crimp bead. Secure crimp bead. Hide tail in beads.

Gold & Gray Watch - MATERIALS: 6 Jet ¼" x 9/16" rectangle glass beads • 4 Jet oval glass beads • 18 Jet 6mm round glass beads • 12 Gun Metal bugle beads • Gold watch • 2 Gold crimp beads • Gold lobster claw clasp • Gold 6mm split ring • 2 Gold coil crimps • Tiger tail • Wire cutters • Crimp pliers

TIPS: Remove watchband. Place coil crimps over watch spring pin. Replace pins in watch. On both sides of watch, thread and center 12" of tiger tail through coil crimps. Pass tiger tail through rectangle bead from opposite sides crossing inside the bead. Thread a round bead on each strand of tiger tail. Pass tiger tail through an oval bead from opposite sides crossing inside the bead. Thread a round bead on each strand of tiger tail. Continue in this manner placing 3 rectangle and 2 oval beads on each side of watch. Finish each strand with 3 bugle beads. Thread both strands through one round bead. Use a crimp bead to attach tiger tail to clasp and split ring.

Pink Flower Pendant Necklace - MATERIALS: 4 Pink engraved heart glass beads • 31 beads from Pink Assortment • 24 Silver metal 2.5mm x 6mm spacer beads • Hirschberg Schutz cable necklace with clasp and chain • ¾" Clear mylar circle • Silver head pin • Wire cutters • Round-nose pliers • Crimp pliers • GOOP Adhesive

TIPS: Glue 4 heart beads on mylar circle with points together. Insert a head pin through 2 opposite hearts. Form loop in end of head pin. Use loop to attach pendant on cable. Glue small bead in center of hearts. Thread beads and pendant on cable. Attach clasp and chain.

Pink Heart Earrings - MATERIALS: 2 Pink engraved heart glass beads • 4 Glass beads from Pink assortment • 2 Silver metal 2.5mm x 6mm spacer beads • 2 Silver head pins • 2 Silver leverback earrings • Wire cutters • Round-nose pliers

TIPS: Thread beads on head pin. Bend loop in end. Use loop to attach pin to earrings.

Never again worry about finding the perfect accessories for your special occasion clothes… make your own beautiful pieces!

Head Pin Beaded Loop

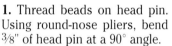

1. Thread beads on head pin. Using round-nose pliers, bend ⅜" of head pin at a 90° angle.

2. Grasp wire end with round-nose pliers and roll down forming a loop. Close loop completely after attaching to bracelet, necklace or earrings.

Purple Choker Necklace - MATERIALS: Amethyst Assortment glass beads • Memory Wire choker • 3 Silver head pins • Clear nail polish • Fine sand paper • Wire cutters • Round-nose pliers

TIPS: Sand ends of Memory Wire and coat with Clear nail polish. Form loop in one end. Thread head pin through rectangle and 2 round beads. Form loop in end. Thread beads and dangle on memory wire. Make loop in opposite end of wire. Make 2 dangles from small beads and head pins. Attach to loops on end of choker.

Purple Drop Earrings - MATERIALS: Amethyst Assortment glass beads (four 4mm, two flat oval, two 8mm faceted) • 2 Silver head pins • 2 Silver fishhook earrings • Wire cutters • Round-nose pliers

TIPS: Thread beads on head pins. Bend loops in ends. Use loop to attach head pin and beads to earrings.

Bead Link

1. Form loop in end of short piece of wire, using round-nose pliers.

2. Thread bead on wire. Trim wire leaving ⅜". Bend wire down and form loop.

Amethyst & Rose Glass Bracelet *by Sarah Berg*

MATERIALS: Amethyst Assortment glass beads • Large Silver bead • Accent beads (size 11° matte Purple, Purple hex) • Heavy beading thread • 2 needles • Beading tray

TIPS: Place 8 matching pairs, single bead and 8 matching pairs of beads on a tray. Cut 72" of thread, thread a needle on each end. String enough Amethyst beads to make a loop around Silver bead, center beads on thread.

Run both threads through a single Amethyst bead. Check to make sure loop fits over Silver bead and adjust beads if necessary.

String all beads for one side on a single strand, then string all the beads for other side on the second strand running both threads through a single bead in the center and through a single bead at the end of the loop.

For Dangle - String several accent beads, 1 large Silver bead and 2 or 3 accent beads on needle. Skip one bead then run thread back through the dangle strand, pull snug.

For Accent beads - Run thread through the bead at the end of the loop. Now work with one strand of thread at a time. Run one thread through 1 bead (come out between 2 beads), add 5 accent beads. Run thread through a bead on the opposite side, add 5 accents beads. Run thread through the next bead on opposite side, add 5 accent beads. Continue in this pattern until you have a single bead above the loop.

Reverse pattern with the second thread, work back to the single bead above the loop (the accent beads will form an 'X' pattern). Tie a good knot.

Run thread through several beads to hide the knot. Tie off thread.

Amethyst & Rose Glass Bracelet Beading Diagrams

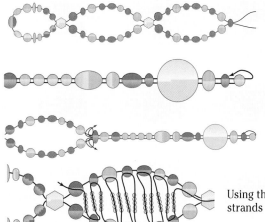

Thread beads for a loop, center on 72" of thread. Thread two 8-bead sets.

Run thread through the end dangle beads, then run thread back through the last dangle bead. Pull snug.

Knot ends of thread around previous threads just above dangle to secure them in place. Tie the ends together in a good knot.

Using the same threads, thread both strands on a single needle. C

Amethyst Earrings -

MATERIALS: Four 8mm faceted glass beads from Amethyst Assortment • 4 Silver metal 4mm beads • 2 Silver head pins • Westrim 12mm Antique Silver floral ear posts with loop

TIPS: Thread the beads on head pins. Bend a loop in end of the head pin. Attach head pin to ear post.

Amethyst Cross Necklace
- MATERIALS: Amethyst Assortment glass beads (two 7/8" diamond shape, nine 6mm faceted) • 5 Silver 2.5mm x 6mm spacer beads • 6 Antique Silver 4mm jump rings • 18" Antique Silver chain necklace • Antique Silver decorative clasp • 20 gauge and 22 gauge Silver wire • Wire cutters • Round-nose pliers • GOOP Adhesive

TIPS: Form closed loop in end of 4" of 20 gauge wire. Thread 3 beads on wire forming top portion of cross. For arms, bend very small loop at center of 3" of 20 gauge wire. Use pliers to flatten loop. Thread cross arms on first wire. Thread 5 beads for lower portion of cross. Push beads together tightly leaving no slack. Trim wire leaving 1/4", bend small loop. Thread beads on cross arms. Trim wire and bend small loops to secure beads. Glue center back of cross to stabilize cross arms. Make 2 wrapped bead links from 22 gauge wire and diamond shaped beads. See page 9. Remove clasp from chain. Cut two 1 1/4" pieces of chain. Use jump rings to attach pieces of chain to both sides of clasp and to bead links. Use jump rings to attach remaining chain to bead links. Use loop at top of cross to attach cross to one portion of clasp. If you cannot find Antique Silver jump rings, use a Black permanent marker to antique Silver jump rings and Silver wire. Color small portions at a time with marker and immediately wipe off with a soft cloth.

Royal Blue Necklace

MATERIALS: Dark Blue Assortment glass beads (five ¾" flat teardrop, six ⅜" teardrop, 17 mushroom) • Hirschberg Schutz Silver cable necklace • 1 Silver 4mm and 4 Silver 6mm jump rings • Silver 12mm lobster claw clasp • 3" of Silver chain • 2 Silver coil crimps • Silver head pin • GOOP Adhesive

TIPS: Thread beads on cable. Glue crimps on ends. Use jump rings to attach clasp and chain. Make dangle with mushroom bead and attach to end of chain.

Royal Blue Earrings

MATERIALS: Six ⅜" teardrop beads from Dark Blue Assortment • 6 Silver 6mm jump rings • 2 Silver fishhook earrings

TIPS: Attach 3 jump rings in a row with one bead on each jump ring.

Crystal Dangle Earrings

MATERIALS: Twenty ³⁄₁₆" flat beads from mini Crystal Assortment • Crystal Assortment glass beads (2 leaf, 4 Small teardrops) • 22 gauge Silver wire • 2 Silver fishhook earrings • 2 Silver 4mm jump rings • 2 Silver toggle clasps • Wire cutters • Round-nose pliers

TIPS: Make 4 bead dangles with 3 flat beads and one teardrop. Make 2 bead dangles with 4 flat beads and one leaf bead. Attach 2 teardrop dangles and one leaf dangle to the round portion of toggle clasp. Use jump ring to attach clasp to earring.

Crystal Choker Necklace

MATERIALS: 44 Crystal glass mini pony beads • 3 leaf and 20 small teardrop glass beads from Crystal Assortment • Eighty ³⁄₁₆" flat beads from Mini Crystal Assortment • Hirschberg Schutz Silver ball choker necklace • 22 gauge Silver wire • Wire cutters • Round-nose pliers

TIPS: Thread a leaf bead on 2" of wire. Bend wire into a triangle loop. Thread 4 mini pony beads. Bend loop in end. Make 3. Make loop in end of twenty 1½" pieces of wire. Attach a teardrop bead to each loop. Thread 3 mini pony beads on 12 of these wires and 4 mini pony beads on 8 wires. Bend loops in ends. Unscrew and remove ball from choker. Thread on 11 mini pony beads. Thread all bead dangles placing a mini pony bead between each one. Finish necklace with 11 mini pony beads. Replace ball on choker.

Bead Dangle

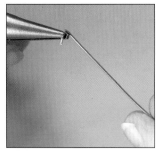

1. Bend wire.

2. Add bead and bend into triangle.

Lime Green Necklace - MATERIALS: Light Green Assortment glass beads (3 teardrops, 23 6mm round) • Lime Green glass bugle beads • Silver metal beads (eleven 4mm, eight 7mm) • 18 gauge Silver wire • 3 Silver head pins • 2 Silver crimp beads • Silver 12mm lobster claw clasp • 3" of Silver chain • Two 20" pieces of tiger tail • Wire cutters • Round-nose pliers • Crimp pliers • Wild Wire Jewelry Jig

TIPS: Following diagram, bend wire on jig. Thread beads on head pins, form loops in ends and attach to wire shape. On each side, fold tiger tail in half through top loop of wire shape. Bring ends of tiger tail together and thread beads. Use crimp bead to attach tiger tail to clasp and chain.

Lime Green Earrings - MATERIALS: 2 glass teardrops from Light Green Assortment • Two 4mm and two 7mm Silver metal beads • 18 gauge Silver wire • 2 Silver head pins • 2 Silver 12mm C-hoop earrings • Wire cutters • Round-nose pliers • Wild Wire Jewelry Jig

TIPS: Form wire shapes on jig. Thread beads on head pin, form loop in end and attach to wire shapes. Thread wire shape on earring.

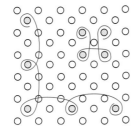

Necklace and Earring Jig Diagram

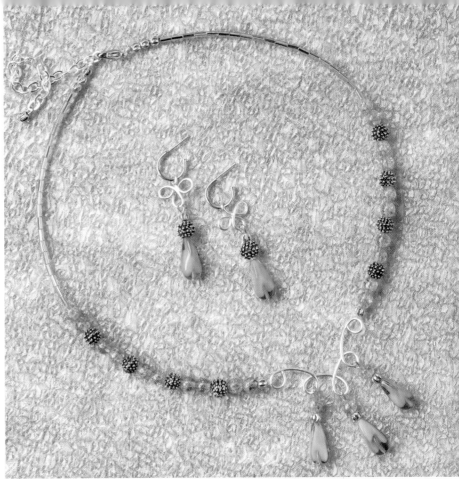

Using a peg jig makes bending your jewelry wire as easy as A-B-C; just follow the diagrams!

Using a Wire Jig

1. Insert pegs in jig following diagram. Wrap wire around pegs. Remove, cut ends flush.

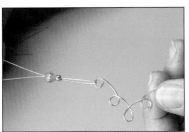

2. Fold tiger tail in half, thread through loop, add beads. **3.** Attach dangles to loops.

Dragonfly Necklace - MATERIALS: 43 Crystal glass mini pony beads • 3 Light Green Assortment triangle glass beads • Silver metal beads (8 Silver dragonfly, four 4mm) • 20 gauge Silver wire • Silver 2-tier cable necklace • 3" of Silver chain • Silver lobster claw clasp • 2 Silver coil crimps • Heavy wire cutters • Round-nose pliers • 1¼" and 1⅞" diameter PVC pipe • GOOP Adhesive

TIPS: Cut one cable from 2-tier cable necklace. Save one strand for later use. Thread Green, Crystal and Silver beads on 2 pieces of wire. Wrap one wire around 1¼" and one around 1⅞" PVC pipe to form circles. Bend loops in ends. Bend loops toward back. Thread beads and shaped wires on cable. Glue crimps on cable ends. Attach clasp and chain with jump rings.

Silver & Crystal Earrings - MATERIALS: 12 Crystal mini pony beads • 2 Silver metal 4mm beads • Silver loop earrings
TIP: Thread beads on loops.

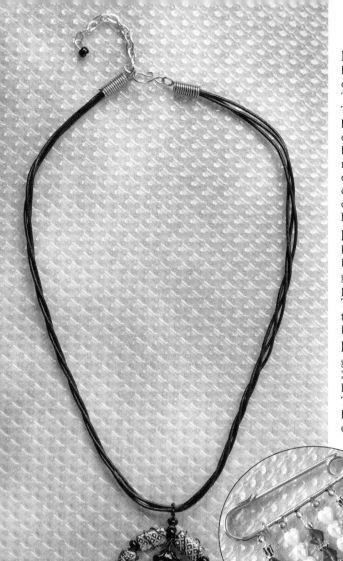

Mask Pendant - MATERIALS: Jet glass beads (mask, six ¼" x ⁹⁄₁₆" rectangle) • 8 Black mini pony beads • 20 gauge Brass and 24 gauge Black wire • Gold head pin • 2" of Gold chain • Three 18" pieces of Black 1mm leather cord • Wild Wire Deluxe Wire Twister • Round-nose pliers • Wire cutters • GOOP Adhesive

TIPS: Thread 6 rectangle beads on Black wire with a mini pony bead between each. Begin and end with wire through a mini pony bead. Fold wire tails up and twist together. Thread a mini pony bead. Form loop above last pony bead. Wrap Black wire around beads in a random pattern. Form a small loop in end of 2" piece of Black wire. Thread mask bead. Bend loop above mask bead. Hang from Black wire in center of circle. Wire ends of 3 leather cords together. Use Twister to twist leather pieces together. Make 2 coiled wire crimps and wire hook clasp with 20 gauge Brass wire. Glue ends of leather cords into coiled wire crimps. Attach chain and hook. Make dangle with pony bead and head pin. Attach to chain.

Red, White and Blue Pin - MATERIALS: Winter Assortment glass beads (2 Red star, 3 Royal Blue mushroom) • 8 Crystal Assortment small White glass heart beads • Silver metal beads (three 8mm x 10mm, three 4mm, two 2.5mm x 6mm) • 20 gauge Silver wire • 2 Silver head pins • Wire cutters • Round-nose pliers • Nylon jaw pliers

TIPS: Thread heart beads and 4mm beads on head pins. Form loops in ends. Attach to charm pin. Make small spirals on ends of 3 pieces of wire leaving 2" tails. Thread beads on wire, form loops in wire ends and attach to charm pin.

Flower Pin - MATERIALS: Aqua ⅝" glass flower bead • 3 Light Green Assortment glass leaf beads • Sea Breeze Assortment faceted glass beads (two 8mm, two 6mm) • 2 Kelly Green twisted glass bugle beads • Silver charm pin • 3 Silver eye pins • 2 Silver head pins • 3 Silver 4mm jump rings • Wire cutters • Round-nose pliers

TIPS: Thread flower and bugle beads on eye pins. Thread faceted beads on head pins. Form loops in ends of pins. Use loops to attach pins to charm pin. Thread leaf beads on jump rings and attach to bottom of eye pins.

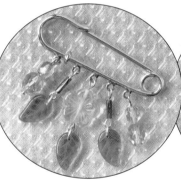

Black Mask Pin - MATERIALS: 3 Black glass mask beads • 6 Jet Assortment glass beads • 5 Gold head pins • Gold charm pin • Wire cutters • Round-nose pliers

TIPS: Thread beads on pins, form loops in ends and attach to charm pin.

Copper & Black Necklace - MATERIALS: 16 Black/Copper glitter oval glass beads • Jet Assortment glass beads (21 faceted 8mm, 14 rice) • Black mini pony bead • 12mm Silver lobster claw clasp • 8 Silver head pins • 2 Silver crimp beads • 3" of Silver chain • 20" of tiger tail • Wire cutters

TIPS: Use crimp bead to attach clasp to one end of tiger tail. Thread faceted beads on 8 head pins. Form loop in ends. Thread beads on tiger tail placing head pin loops between 2 faceted beads. Use crimp bead to attach chain to opposite end of tiger tail. Thread mini pony bead on head pin, bend loop in end and attach to chain.

Copper and Black Earrings - MATERIALS: 2 Black/Copper glitter oval glass beads • 6 Jet Assortment Black 8mm faceted glass beads • 2 Black seed beads • 2 Silver earring dangles • 8 Silver head pins • 2 Silver 4mm jump rings • 2 Silver fishhook earrings • Wire cutters • Round-nose pliers

TIPS: Thread faceted beads on 6 head pins. Cut head pins leaving ⅜" above bead. Form loop in end. Attach a faceted bead to lower loops on dangle. Thread seed and oval beads on 2 head pins. Bend a loop in end and attach to upper loop on dangles. Use jump ring to attach dangle to earring.

Silver Rings Necklace - MATERIALS: 26 Jet mushroom beads • One flat oval Jet bead • 30 Silver metal 3mm x 8mm tube beads • 18 gauge Silver wire • Silver toggle clasp • 2 Silver crimp beads • Silver head pin • Silver 6mm jump ring • 22" of tiger tail • PVC pipe (1", 1¼", 1½") • Wire cutters • Round-nose pliers • Crimp pliers

TIPS: Use crimp bead to attach one end of tiger tail to half of clasp. Thread beads. Use crimp bead to attach end of tiger tail to other half of clasp. Wrap wire around PVC pipe to form 1", 1¼" and 1½" circles. See page 17. Insert and glue ends of wire circles in tube beads. Thread oval bead on head pin. Form loop in end. Place wire circles and oval bead on jump ring. Attach to center of necklace.

Silver Rings Earrings - MATERIALS: 2 Jet glass oval beads • 2 Silver metal 3mm x 8mm tube beads • 18 gauge wire • 2 Silver head pins • 2 Silver fishhook earrings • 2 Silver 4mm jump rings • Wire cutters • Round-nose pliers • 1" PVC pipe

TIPS: Wrap the wire around the PVC pipe to form two 1" circles. Insert and glue ends of circles in tube beads. Thread the oval beads on the head pins. Form loop. Attach wire circle and oval bead to the earring with a jump ring.

Closure Detail

Wrapped Wire Link

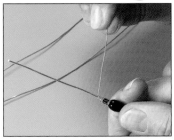

Form loop 1½" from end of 4" wire. Wrap wire tail around wire 4 or 5 times. Cut end flush with wire. Thread bead on wire. Bend a loop leaving ¼" of bare wire between bead and loop. Wrap tail around wire 4 or 5 times. Cut end flush with wire. Straighten loops.

Wrapped Loops

1. Make loops in ends of 18 gauge wires.

2. Wrap with 26 gauge wire.

From casual leather and 'safety pin' projects to elegant wrapped wire bracelets and earrings, there's a design for every taste!

Silver & Black Wrap Bracelet

MATERIALS: Jet Assortment glass beads (one ⅝" diamond, two ⅜" oval) • Silver metal tube beads (two 7mm, two 8mm x 10mm) • 18 gauge and 26 gauge Silver wire • Wire cutters • Round-nose pliers • Nylon jaw pliers

TIPS: Cut three 7" pieces of 18 gauge wire. Center beads on one wire. Insert the end of a 2" piece of 26 gauge wire into the last bead on each side. Wrap wire tightly around 18 gauge wire. Form loops in the ends of three 7" wires and shape into matching ovals. Holding the wires together, wrap 26 gauge wire around the 3 wires close to loops. Skip ½" and wrap again.

Silver & Black Earrings

MATERIALS: Jet Assortment glass beads (two ⅜" oval, 2 small teardrop) • Silver metal beads (two 8mm x 10mm, two 7mm) • 2 Silver 7mm jump rings • 2 Silver eye pins • 2 Silver fishhook earrings

TIPS: Thread beads on eye pins. Form loop in end of eye pins. Attach eye pins to earrings. Thread teardrop beads on jump rings and attach to loops on bottom of eye pins.

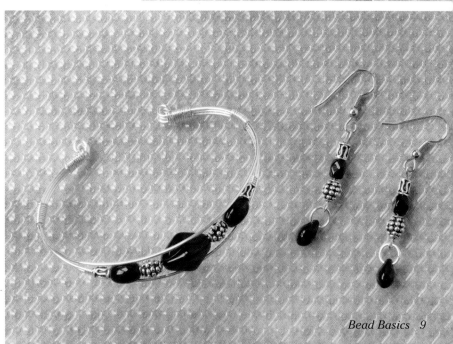

Bead Basics 9

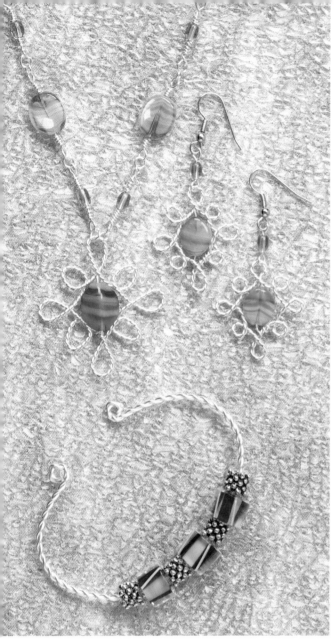

Looped Blue Pendant Necklace - MATERIALS: Light Blue Assortment glass beads (3 large oval, 8 small drum) • 22 gauge Silver wire • Silver link chain with clasp • 12 Silver 4mm jump rings • Wild Wire Jewelry Jig • Wild Wire Deluxe Wire Twister • Wire cutters • Round-nose pliers • GOOP Adhesive
TIPS: Following manufacturer's instructions, fold 30" of wire in half and twist together. Place pegs in jig following diagram. Bend wire shape leaving a straight piece of wire in center to hold bead. Place GOOP in oval bead and thread bead on straight wire. Make 10 wrapped wire bead links. Use jump rings to attach 5 links on each side of pendant. Attach chain to last link on each side. . (see jig instructions on page 7)

Looped Blue Earrings - MATERIALS: Light Blue Assortment glass beads (2 large oval, 2 small drum) • Two 10" pieces of 22 gauge Silver wire • 2 Silver fishhook earrings • Wild Wire Jewelry Jig • Wire cutters • Round-nose pliers
TIPS: Following instructions for necklace, twist wire, bend shape, make bead link and attach to earring. (see jig instructions on page 7)

Blue Twisted Bracelet - MATERIALS: 3 Striped Blue glass beads • 4 Silver metal drum beads • 20" of Silver 18 gauge wire • Wild Wire Deluxe Wire Twister • Wire cutters • Round-nose pliers • GOOP Adhesive
TIPS: Following manufacturer's instructions, fold wire in half and tightly twist. Shape into oval. Cut away excess wire. Thread beads. Bend loops in wire ends. Glue last bead on each side.

Necklace Jig Diagram   Earring Jig Diagram

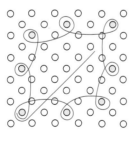

𝒯wisted 𝒲ire

You will love the results that twisted wire gives your jewelry pieces. Your friends and family will be in awe at your creative ability.

1. Bend a piece of wire in half, thread fold in hook and secure

ends in clamp or tie around a cabinet handle. Hold tool in one hand, pull wire taut and rotate handle with other hand. **2.** Cut wire to desired length and make loop in end. **3.** Thread on beads. Make loop in other end of twisted wire.

Turquoise & Black Drop Necklace - MATERIALS: 16 Black glass mini pony beads • 12 Jet Assortment oval glass beads • 5 Sea Breeze Assortment Turquoise and Black teardrop glass beads • 14 Silver metal 4mm x 6mm oval beads • Silver cable necklace • 12mm Silver lobster clasp • 5 Silver head pins • 2 Silver 4mm jump rings • 2 Silver coil crimps • 3" of Silver chain • 20 gauge Silver wire • 7/8" PVC pipe • Wire cutters • Round-nose pliers • GOOP Adhesive
TIPS: Shape four 2¼" pieces of wire by wrapping around PCV pipe. See page 17. Thread one mini pony bead and 2 Silver beads on each piece. Bend loops in wire ends. Bend loops to back. Thread teardrop beads on 5 head pins for dangles. Form loop in ends of head pins. Thread wire scallops, dangles and beads on cable. Place 2 Black oval beads between loops of scallops. Glue coil crimps on cable ends and attach chain and clasp to crimps.

Turquoise & Black Earrings - MATERIALS: 2 Sea Breeze Assortment Turquoise and Black teardrop glass beads • 6 Black glass mini pony beads • 2 Silver metal 4mm x 6mm oval beads • 2 Silver 12mm jump rings • 2 Silver head pins • 2 Silver fishhook earrings
TIPS: Thread teardrop, Silver and pony bead on head pin. Form loop in end of head pin. Thread head pin on jump ring with a Black bead on each side. Attach jump ring.

All shades of blue, from the hues of a sparkling pool to the color of the sky at twilight, can be found in these unusual pieces!

Blue Heart Necklace - MATERIALS: 10 Black/Blue/White square glass beads • Jet Assortment 10mm faceted glass bead • Light Blue Assortment heart glass bead • 15 Silver metal drum beads • Silver head pin • Silver S hook clasp • 2 Silver coil crimps • 2 Silver 7mm jump rings • 22" of 1mm Black leather cord • Wire cutters • Round-nose pliers • GOOP Adhesive
TIPS: Thread heart, Silver and Black bead on head pin. Shape loop in end of head pin. Thread beads on cord with heart bead dangle in center. Thread coil crimp on cord ends. Fold loops in cord ends, slide coil crimp over cord ends, glue to secure. Add the clasp.

Blue Heart Earrings - MATERIALS: 2 Light Blue Assortment heart glass beads • 2 Jet Assortment 10mm faceted glass beads • 2 Silver metal drum beads • 2 Silver head pins • 2 Silver 12mm C-hoop earrings • Wire cutters • Round-nose pliers
TIPS: Thread heart, Silver and Black beads on head pins. Form small loop in end of head pins. Slide head pins on earrings.

Jump Rings

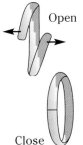

Open

Close

Open and close your jump rings side to side using needle-nose pliers.

1. To make jump rings, wrap wire around rod with wraps close together.

2. Remove coil from rod and cut coil apart one loop at a time. Open jump ring by bending ends to the side. Do not pull ends apart.

Aqua Link Bracelet - MATERIALS: 34 Aqua glass mini pony beads • Silver toggle clasp • Jump rings (17 Silver 10mm, 19 Silver 4mm)
TIPS: Thread 2 beads on each 10mm jump ring. Use 4mm jump rings to connect 10mm jump rings. Use 4mm jump rings to attach clasp on each end.

Aqua Hoop Earrings
MATERIALS: 12 Aqua glass mini pony beads • 4 Silver metal 2.5mm x 6mm spacer beads • Silver hoop earrings
TIP: Thread beads on earrings.

Amber Flower Pendant is Fun to Make!

Pendants transform plain necklaces into just plain gorgeous! Mahogany assortment and black beads give the projects the look of amber and jet.

Amber Pendant -

MATERIALS: Mahogany Assortment glass beads (5 Amber 4mm diamonds) • Black glass mini pony beads • Black seed beads • 20 gauge Brass wire • 18" of 2mm Gold cord • Wild Wire Twister • Wire cutters • Round-nose pliers • GOOP Adhesive

TIPS: Cut five $1\frac{1}{8}$" pieces of Brass wire. Form loops in one end. Thread diamond bead on each wire. Form loops in ends. Thread a piece of Brass wire through 5 loops. Pull tight and twist wire forming 5 point star. Make a loop in one end of 8" of Brass wire. Shape into a circle. Thread shaped wire through loops on star placing 8 or 9 mini pony beads between each star point. Thread wire end through beginning loop and bend up at a right angle. Form a loop. Glue 4mm bead in center of star. Attach star pendant to center of cord. Thread seed beads on Brass wire. Using Wire Twister's large metal rod, wrap $\frac{1}{4}$" of bare wire. Bring seed beads up. Wrap seed beads and wire around rod 4 or 5 times. Wrap $\frac{1}{4}$" of bare wire to finish. Make 6 of these beads. Thread 3 on each side of necklace. Glue to secure. Make 2 coil crimps and hook clasp from Brass wire. Glue cord ends into crimps. Attach clasp.

Hook Clasp

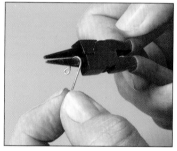 

1. Make a hook clasp with wire.
2. Bend a very small loop in one end of a $1\frac{3}{8}$" piece of wire. Use round-nose pliers to grasp wire just below loop. Place wire half way down the shank of pliers. Bend wire around shank of pliers. Form a loop in the end of wire in opposite direction than first loop.

Seed Bead Coil

1. Thread seed beads on wire and wrap $\frac{1}{4}$" of bare wire around rod.

2. Bring beads up and wrap around rod 4 to 5 times.

3. Finish by wrapping $\frac{1}{4}$" of bare wire around rod.

Beaded jewelry never goes out of style!

Spiral with Bead

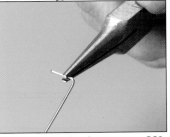

1. Bend end of wire at 90°. Thread on bead.

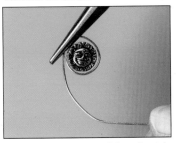

2. Roll wire around bead with pliers.

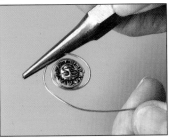

3. Continue making spiral around bead.

Topaz Necklace

MATERIALS: Mahogany Assortment glass beads (5 Light Topaz, 4 Dark Topaz) • One large and 8 small Silver metal sun beads • Topaz seed beads • 18" of 20 gauge Silver wire • 12mm Silver lobster claw clasp • 4mm and 6mm Silver jump rings • 2 Silver crimp beads • 22" of tiger tail • Wire cutters • Round-nose pliers • Nylon jaw pliers • GOOP Adhesive

TIPS: Bend 3/8" of wire end up at 90°. Place GOOP in hole of large sun bead. Insert wire end into bead. Allow adhesive to set. Using nylon jaw pliers to grasp wire, form a closed spiral around sun bead. When spiral is 1 1/4" wide, bend wire end up at a right angle. Thread a Topaz bead. Bend loop in wire end. Use crimp and 4mm jump ring to attach clasp to one end of tiger tail. Thread 6 1/2" of seed beads on tiger tail. Thread Topaz beads, small sun beads and pendant on tiger tail. Add 6 1/2" of seed beads. Use crimp bead to attach tiger tail to 6mm jump ring.

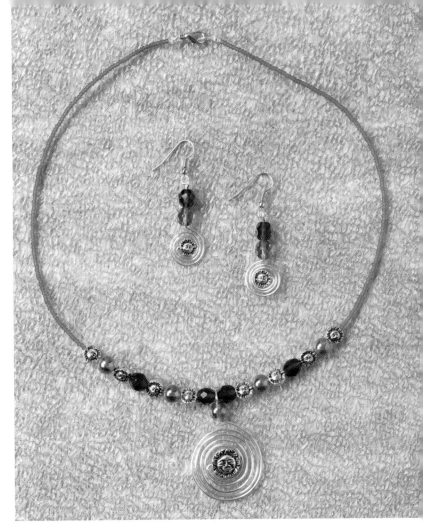

Topaz Sun Bead Earrings - MATERIALS: Mahogany Assortment glass beads (2 Light Topaz, 2 Dark Topaz) • 2 small Silver metal sun beads • Two 9" pieces of Silver 20 gauge wire • 2 Silver fishhook earrings • Wire cutters • Round-nose pliers • Nylon jaw pliers • GOOP Adhesive

TIPS: Bend 1/4" of wire end up at 90°. Place GOOP in hole of small sun bead. Insert wire end into bead. Allow adhesive to set. Using nylon jaw pliers to grasp wire, form a closed spiral around sun bead. When spiral is 5/8" wide, bend wire end up at 90°. Thread 2 beads. Bend loop in wire end. Use loop to attach spiral to earring.

Amber Choker Necklace - MATERIALS: Dark Topaz seed beads • Mahogany Assortment glass beads (sixteen 8mm, five flat oval, four 6mm, one square) • Two 17" pieces of Memory Wire • 2 Gold 4mm jump rings • 22 gauge Gunmetal wire • Wire cutters • Round-nose pliers

TIPS: Make 8 bead links consisting of two 8mm beads with loops on both ends. Bend loop in end of one piece of Memory Wire. Thread on seed beads. Center bead links on Memory Wire placing 6 seed beads between each bead link. Finish top row with seed beads. Bend loop in end of Memory wire. Make 5 oval bead dangles with loops on both ends. Bend a loop in one end of second piece of Memory Wire. Thread seed beads. Center oval bead dangles on Memory Wire placing 6 seed beads and lower loop links between each dangle. Finish with seed beads and a loop in end of Memory Wire. Make four 6mm bead dangles and one square bead dangle with loops on both ends. Attach to oval bead dangles. Thread jump rings through end loops of Memory Wire to connect strands.

Amber Coiled Earrings - MATERIALS: 2 Mahogany Assortment teardrop glass beads • Dark Topaz seed beads • 2 Gold fishhook earrings • 22 gauge Gun Metal wire

TIPS: Make a small loop in end of 6" of wire. Thread teardrop bead then seed beads. Wrap wire and seed beads around a pencil. Stretch coils slightly. Bend loop in end and attach to earrings.

Closure
Detail

Multi Color Cross Pendant - MATERIALS: 9 Round multi color glass beads • 2 tube multi color glass beads • 6mm jump ring • 18 and 22 gauge Gun Metal wire • 20" of 1mm Black cord • Wild Wire Wonder • Wire cutters • Round-nose pliers • GOOP Adhesive

TIPS: Form closed loop in end of 4" of 18 gauge wire. Thread 2 beads on wire forming top portion of cross. To form arms of cross, bend very small loop at center of a 3" piece of 18 gauge wire. Use pliers to flatten loop. Thread cross arms on first wire. Thread 3 beads for lower portion of cross. Push beads together tightly leaving no slack. Trim wire leaving ¼". Bend small loop. Thread beads on cross arms. Trim wire and bend small loops to secure beads. Glue center back of cross to stabilize cross arms. Wrap 22 gauge wire around and over beads in a random pattern. Hide wire ends in beads. Thread and center cross on cord. Wrap 22 gauge wire around small metal twister rod. Place each wrap against the previous wrap. Make 2 wire coils. Stretch center of coils and insert tube beads. Thread one on each side of cord. Glue to secure. Make a hook clasp with 22 gauge wire. Wrap 22 gauge wire around large metal twister rod and make 2 wire coils. Bend last coil on one end up at a right angle to form loop. Thread a coil on each cord end. Thread jump ring on one end. Fold cord over and insert end into coil. Glue to secure. Attach hook to cord loop.

Black & Multi Color Necklace

MATERIALS: Black glass mini pony beads • 5 large glass beads • 10 7mm Silver metal beads • 2 Silver crimp beads • Antique Silver hook and clasp • Three 24" pieces of tiger tail • Crimp pliers • Wire cutters

TIPS: Use a crimp bead to attach 3 pieces of tiger tail to one portion of clasp. Treating the 3 wires as one, thread 5" of mini pony beads. Add one large bead with a Silver bead on each side. Separate strands of tiger tail. Thread 10 mini pony beads on each strand. Bring strands back together and thread one large bead with a Silver bead on each side. Continue in this manner. Finish with 5" of mini pony beads. Use crimp bead to attach second portion of clasp to the 3 strands of tiger tail.

Coiled Crimps

1. Insert wire end through the 2 holes in the handle of Wild Wire Wonder. Press wire against rod with thumb and finger of one hand. Use other hand to twist handle placing each wrap against the previous wrap.

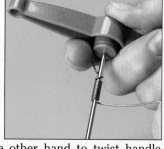

2. Bend last loop up at a 90° angle and trim wire ends for loop.

3. Bend loop. Attach clasp or jump ring to this loop. Glue coiled crimps on ends of cord or cable. The last coil on bottom of crimps can

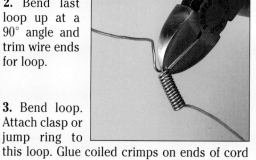

be compressed to help hold cord or cable.

Multi Color Necklace -

MATERIALS: Glass beads (12 tube, six 10mm, eight 6mm, 7 oval) • Silver metal (twenty-six 6mm x 7mm, twelve 4mm) • 3" of Silver chain • 18 gauge Silver wire • 12mm Silver lobster claw clasp • Silver head pin • 2 Silver crimp beads • 22" of tiger tail • Wire cutters • Round-nose pliers • Nylon jaw pliers

TIPS: For dangles, make 7 small wire spirals with 2" tails. Thread 6mm and oval beads on each one. Make a loop in wire end. Use crimp bead to attach tiger tail to clasp. Thread six 4mm Silver on wire. Add remaining beads and dangles as shown in photo and end with six 4mm Silver beads. Use crimp bead to attach chain to other end of tiger tail. Thread a 6mm bead on head pin. Bend loop in end. Attach to end of chain.

Earrings - MATERIALS:

Two 6mm and two 10mm glass beads • 2 Silver metal 6mm x 7mm beads • 2 Silver fishhook earrings • 18 gauge Silver wire • Wire cutters • Round-nose pliers • Nylon jaw pliers

TIPS: Make 2 small wire spirals with 2" tails. Thread beads. Make loops in ends. Attach to earrings.

Showcase handmade beads on designs with an ethnic flavor. Make your own coil crimps and wire spirals or add a tassel to complete the project!

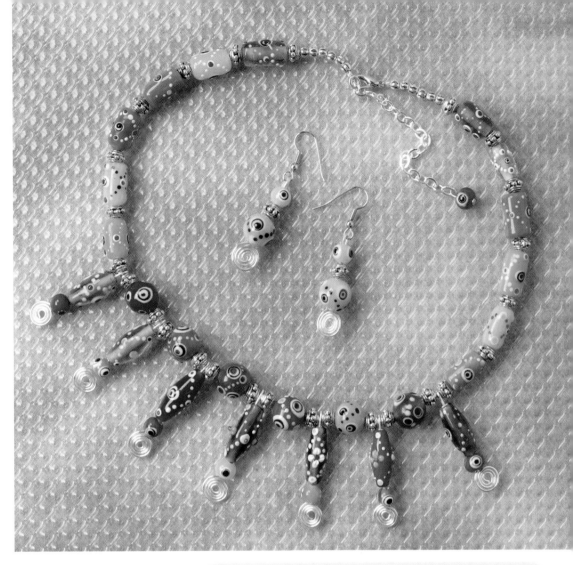

Multi Color Tassel Bracelet - MATERIALS: 6 small and 6 medium round glass beads • 13 Silver metal 8mm x 10mm beads • 1½" Navy Blue tassel • 9" of Stretch Magic beading cord

TIPS: Thread a Silver bead on tassel cord. Thread beads and tassel on stretch cord. To finish, tie cord in a square knot. Hide knot in medium glass bead.

Wire Spirals

1. Form a loop at end of wire with round-nose pliers.

2. Reposition the pliers and bend wire again.

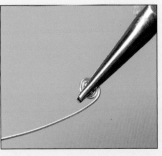

3. Continue until the spiral is required size. Spiral can be tight or loose.

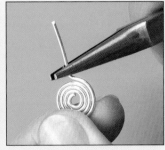

4. Bend end up at a 90° angle.

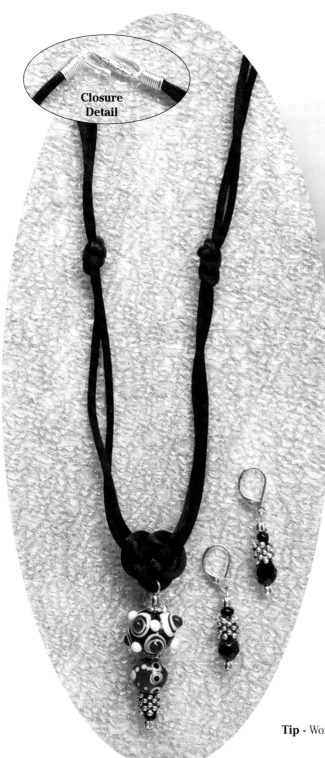

Closure
Detail

Red, White & Blue Bracelet

MATERIALS: 6 large Red/White/Blue round glass beads • 12 Dark Blue Assortment small Blue spacer glass beads • 7 Red Assortment mushroom glass beads • 9" of tiger tail • Silver toggle clasp • 2 Silver crimp beads • 1" of Silver chain

TIPS: Use crimp bead to attach tiger tail to round portion of clasp. Thread beads as shown. Attach chain to bar portion of clasp. Use crimp bead to attach tiger tail to chain.

Combine Red with Black or Blue for a sophisticated Oriental inspired necklace and a patriotic bracelet.

Red & Black Pendant

MATERIALS: Large and small glass beads • Black mini pony bead • Silver metal beads (two 4mm, two 2.5mm x 6mm, drum bead) • Silver head pin • Silver S clasp • 2 Silver coil crimps • Two 30" pieces of Black rattail cord • Wire cutters • Round-nose pliers • GOOP Adhesive

TIPS: Following diagram, tie a Shamrock Knot in the center of 2 cords. Tie an Overhand Knot on each side 4" above the center knot. Glue coil crimps to ends of cord. Thread clasp through loops of coiled crimp. Thread beads on head pin. Bend loop in end of head pin. Attach to center knot.

Black & Silver Earrings

MATERIALS: 2 Black 8mm glass faceted beads • 2 Black glass mini pony beads • Silver metal beads (four 4mm, 2 drum) • 2 Silver head pins • 2 Silver leverback earrings • Wire cutters • Round-nose pliers

TIPS: Thread beads on head pins. Bend loop in end of head pins. Attach to earrings.

Diagrams for Shamrock Knot

Tip - Work on a soft board so you can pin cords in place temporarily.

Note: - Tie the knot with 2 strands of cord.

Overhand
Knot
for sides of
necklace

Knots create an unusual touch on this Red & Black Pendant!

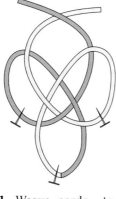

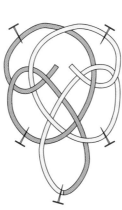

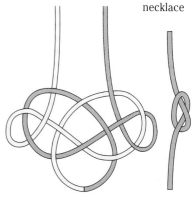

1. Weave cords to look like the diagram.

2. Continue to weave the ends of the cord.

3. Finish weaving cords like the diagram.

4. Remove all pins then pull cords gently until they are snug to form a secure knot (see photo).

Shaped Wire

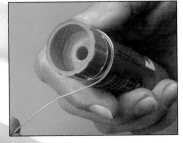

1. Shape wire by wrapping around PVC pipe.

2. Thread the beads and make loops in the ends.

3. Hold in fingers as shown and bend the loops to the back.

Show your colors... Red, White & Blue forever!

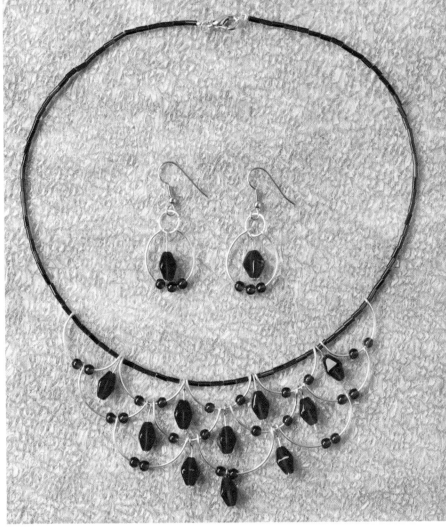

Red Three Tier Necklace - MATERIALS: Red Assortment glass beads (10 large Red diamond, 24 Red 4mm) • Red bugle beads • 12mm Silver lobster claw clasp • 2 Silver 6mm jump rings • 10 Silver head pins • 2 Silver crimp beads • 22" of tiger tail • 20 gauge Silver wire • 7/8" PVC pipe • Wire cutters • Round-nose pliers

TIPS: Shape five 2" pieces of wire by wrapping around PVC pipe. Thread two 4mm beads on each piece. Bend a loop in each wire end toward the back. Thread diamond beads on head pins for dangles. Bend loop in ends 1/4" from bead. Use crimp bead to attach clasp to one end of tiger tail. Thread on 6" of bugle beads. Thread 5 wire scallops placing 5 bugle beads between the loops of each scallop and one dangle pin between scallops. Thread 6" of bugle beads on tiger tail. Use crimp bead to attach tiger tail to jump ring. For second tier, shape four 2 1/4" pieces of wire around PVC pipe. Add two 4mm beads and bend loops in ends. Attach each scallop between 4mm beads on first tier. Attach a dangle between each scallop. For third tier, shape three 2 3/8" pieces of wire around PVC pipe. Add beads, form loops and attach between 4mm beads on second tier. Attach the dangles between each scallop and to the center scallop.

Red Tier Earrings - MATERIALS: Red Assortment glass beads (2 diamond, six 4mm) • 2 Silver 10mm jump rings • 2 Silver head pins • 2 Silver fishhook earrings • 20 gauge Silver wire • 7/8" PVC pipe • Wire cutters • Round-nose pliers

TIPS: Shape two 2 1/2" pieces of wire around PVC pipe. Thread on three 4mm beads. Bend loops in ends. Thread large beads on head pins for dangles. Bend loops in ends. Thread wire scallop and dangle on jump ring. Attach jump ring to earrings.

Red & Silver Charm Bracelet - MATERIALS: 5 Red teardrops and 10 Red 8mm faceted glass beads from Red Assortment • 10 Crystal mini glass pony beads • 10 Silver metal drum beads • 5 Hirschberg Schutz Silver heart clasps • 5 Silver head pins • 5 Silver 7mm jump rings • 9" of Stretch Magic Beading cord • Round-nose pliers

TIPS: Thread teardrop beads on head pins. Form loops in ends. Attach jump rings to hearts. Thread beads, head pins and hearts on cord as shown. To finish, tie cord in a square knot. Hide knot inside a Silver bead.

Green Lariat Necklace

MATERIALS: Dark Green glass mini pony beads • 12 Light Green Assortment glass flower beads • Sea Breeze Assortment glass beads (12 Dark Green disk, 6 Light Green 8mm faceted, 6 Dark Green 8mm faceted) • One ½" and two ³⁄₁₆" Green and Black stripe square glass beads • Silver metal beads (fourteen 6mm, two 4mm, 12 tiny drum) • 40" of tiger tail • Silver head pin • Silver crimp bead • Crimp pliers • Wire cutters • Round-nose pliers • GOOP Adhesive

TIPS: Stack square beads. Turn beads at different angles and glue together. Thread beads on head pin as shown. Bend loop at top to make dangle. Center 22 mini pony beads on tiger tail. Bring ends of tiger tail together and thread one mini pony bead. Thread beads repeating pattern 6 times. Thread a crimp bead then dangle. Thread tiger tail back through crimp bead. Pull beads tight and compress crimp. Thread ends in beads to hide.

Tiger Tail Wire

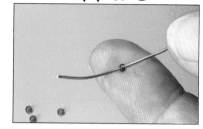

Thread seed beads on tiger tail.

Green Dangle Earrings

MATERIALS: 42 Dark Green glass mini pony beads • 2 Dark Green 6mm disk • Silver metal beads (6 tiny drum, two 6mm, two 4mm) • 2 Silver crimp beads • 2 Silver fishhook earrings • 12" of tiger tail • Wire cutters • Crimp pliers

TIPS: Thread beads on tiger tail. Bring ends together and thread on one mini pony bead. Use crimp bead to attach tiger tail to earrings.

Turquoise & Green Bracelet

MATERIALS: 4 Sea Breeze Assortment ³⁄₈" x ⁵⁄₈" glass rectangle beads • 3 Green Assortment ⁷⁄₁₆" x ½" oval glass beads • 7 matte Turquoise ½" glass bugle beads • Peacock Luster seed beads • 13" of fine Silver chain • 2 Silver 4mm jump rings • Silver toggle clasp • 24 gauge Silver wire • Wire cutters • Round-nose pliers • Crimp pliers

TIPS: Cut chain in half. Use jump rings to attach clasp to ends of chain. Cut fourteen 1¼" pieces of wire. Form a very small loop in one end of each piece. Use crimp pliers to compress loop. Thread one seed bead on a wire. Thread wire through chain, add rectangle bead and thread through second chain, add a seed bead and form small loop. Compress loop with crimp pliers. Referring to photo, continue in this manner adding 2 seed beads to oval and rectangle beads and 4 seed beads to bugle beads to make all bead units the same width.

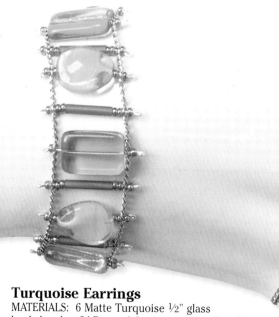

Turquoise Earrings

MATERIALS: 6 Matte Turquoise ½" glass bugle beads • 24 Peacock Luster seed beads • 6 Silver head pins • 2 Silver 4mm jump rings • 2 Silver fishhook earrings • 2 Hirschberg Schutz Silver clasps

TIPS: Thread beads on head pins. Form loops in ends of head pins. Attach to loop half of clasps. Use jump ring to attach clasp to earrings.

Now you can make it yourself!